GYPROCK

BRIAN ECHENBERG

authorHOUSE®

AuthorHouse™
1663 Liberty Drive
Bloomington, IN 47403
www.authorhouse.com
Phone: 833-262-8899

Published by AuthorHouse 12/21/2021

ISBN: 978-1-6655-4756-7 (sc)
ISBN: 978-1-6655-4766-6 (e)

Library of Congress Control Number: 2021925442

Print information available on the last page.

ONE OF MY EARLIEST MEMORIES was of my parents giving us up to caretakers while they were on vacation. I recall the smell of porridge and Jell-O and I must have been above three or four at the time because we lived on Wilson Avenue until I was five. I don't remember a lot but even then it was traumatic. Later on, maybe when I was 4, we had a sadistic woman looking after us kid's, who said don't expect your parents back, they died in a plane crash. I cried and was terror stricken with what this sadistic woman said. Also on Wilson, on the subject of traumatic events, my father and mother had a fight and my father physically pushed my mother down and because of that she was bedridden for a few days. My first experience with marriage was negative and marked by violent physical contact.

We were crying when we witnessed this event on Wilson Ave. when I was five. And when I had to start grade one and go to school I was terrified too and didn't want to go. I stood in the bathtub and refused. I was scared a lot and finally went to the wrong classroom and was mixed up, I finally found the right classroom and sat there picking my nose and remember the teacher calling me a pig. I couldn't find the right locker either. On the subject of traumatic thoughts much later in high school when I was about 14 I was obsessed with two things in three years. The first was caused by backing out of a fight with Peter in the stairway. I instigated the fight and when I found out it was to be a fistfight instead of wrestling, which I was more used to, I called the fight off.

For years after, I was super worried about my manhood and couldn't stop ruminating about it it as it was a disaster for me. The second obsession was how to physically have intercourse and this one lasted until four years later when I actually overcame this torture by sleeping with Barbara in New Jersey. These two facets of obsessive thinking, fighting and screwing, were torture for me. They consumed all my waking hours. Of all the traumatic experiences the one at home on alpine was the worst, when my mother gave away my precious Daschund Blackie which I never got over. He Peed on her precious drapes and that was the last straw. I love dogs and used to draw them. But the anger and hurt had no relief I remember. I even found 50 years later, swimming at the Y, an older woman who was probably my teacher in kindergarten, because the time frame made sense. She mentioned and remembered the owners of my house on Beaconsfield, had 2 Scotties and made a wooden Scottie address number which I never altered even with all the transformations and renovations my house on Beaconsfield went through. A little later I went to Hebrew school and was so clued out in 5 years I wasn't aware I would graduate soon. I just joked around with my friends Larry and Ronnie heir and learned nothing.

I was the class clown, a pattern which would be repeated

through my life. Maybe I had a learning disability even then. For my bar mitzvah I studied with Cantor Leibovitz to learn to read my parts and was scared to actually perform it. That night people came over to the house and showered me with money and gifts and I was excited with the company. Before that I remember my brothers bar mitzvah and when people came over Donald stayed in his room and didn't socialize. But I was more outgoing and loved the attention. About this time, before and after, I loved going out for supper with my parents and even loved when we went on vacation to places like Florida for Easter and old Orchard for the last week of August, the end of school vacation. Donald didn't like to go to Old Orchard and would throw up in the car. He didn't like to travel. I was more adventurous and excited than him about it. He would say, "Why do we need to go anywhere when we can stay here"? but I always loved to go. Also when we were fighting, me and my brother, he would always win except for one time at the cottage I tried and exerted myself to my fullest extent and came out on top. I remember that because I felt it was an accomplishment as he was two years older and bigger and stronger.

The country was where I went every summer and I never went to camp, but Donald was picked to go to camp Arrowhead for one month, not me though. Even to the present day I am faced with Donald in my dreams and he is markedly stronger than me and I can never come out on top. My biggest joy though was to go out for supper with my parents or just my father and maybe Donald. One time with my mother she took me out for lunch and when I was ordering she said why feed you, you just shit it out anyway. When I was about 20 a girl named Lori from Massachusetts came to visit and stay over at Alpine which resulted in a huge embarrassment, which was really to be expected.

My mother threw her out of the ground floor guestroom and told her "You're leaving today and you're not staying any longer ". To have my mother out of control that way and trying to throw Lori out was something I'll always remember. She did the same thing with Barbara later on and complained to her "You don't know how to use the washing machine stop using it "and kicked her out. Another girl my mother took a vicious dislike to what is Audrey. Audrey liked my father but her hatred of my mother was mutual. My father read the Jewish news which Audrey liked and over which they bonded. I don't think my mother ever met Audrey but she hated her. Audrey had a green gremlin car which was her handle on the short wave radio she would use. Sharing this experience with girlfriends and my mother, my brother's girlfriend Helen brought out a vicious hatred by my mother even though she never met her. My mother made Donald's life a living hell over Helen and Libby kept after Donald relentlessly. Donald went so far as taking Libby's Chevy nova to old orchard with Helen without Libby's knowledge.

A psychologist could make a lot out of Libby's dislike of any of her son's girlfriends and affection towards other women. I don't know why I lived so long, till 27 years old in this situation on alpine. I only left when she threw me out by changing the locks on the door and calling the police to escort me out. I never left willingly, even with the abuse and when I worked at Ogilvy's she had lawyers come to where I worked beseeching me to move out, In front of my coworkers. Very embarrassing! Libby was definitely not in her right mind, illustrated by all these reactions to my father Donald and me. She was definitely of control when I was growing up and especially during my adolescence. When she threw me out my father was in Florida and said he cried when he heard the news. During that period of my life I would take refuge in the basement with my stereo, guitar and pedal steel guitar. It was also cool down there and I could take refuge. My pedal steel guitar needed constant mechanical attention and uncharacteristically, I became handy with it. I rigged up levers and wire connectors to make it work as well as painting it. I'd go to Pascal's hardware to buy rods and nails to rig up the pitch changing devices. One of my obsessions, the one having sex the first time, ended soon after this time. Barbara Wollner, who took my virginity at the tender age of 24, greatly helped me getting over that. She is out of touch with me now.

When I visited her in New Jersey for two weeks, I cheated on her boyfriend Brian, to accomplish this. I went to New York City by train to Grand Central Station and phoned her from there. She immediately invited me to visit her in her apartment. It was there I experienced freedom away from my family situation on alpine. I had fun, went to the beach, and went to her brother's graduation in Philadelphia as well as consuming beer under a very hot summer sun in New Jersey. And lost my virginity finally after worrying about it for five years of torment. I visited Barbara again at her friend's chalet in New Hampshire. I was very nervous and upset and I returned home to get a letter saying "your nervousness and insecurity really got to me and I'm saying goodbye." Jerry, my best friend at the time and his wife Lila, fixed me up with her and we partied and went to the country with our guitars and Frisbees. This was when we were in our early 20s and I had no direction and was interested only in playing guitar, which I was good at. Sir George Williams university, from which I graduated in 1974, was a big party and me and Jerry rented an apartment on Overdale for $27 each a month.

I got the money using the money my father gave me for books which was spend on rent and dope and beer. Everything in school was an excuse to party with my friends, but I was getting paranoid as a result of hash and acid. Listening to Music at that time, and playing guitar, was our main interest and we were constantly doing it. Guitar was evidently my sphere of talent and ability and everywhere, in our apartment and hash hall, were where we would jam and get stoned and get drunk. Jerry, Larry, me, Emil, and all the others spent our time playing guitar and smoking dope and drinking beer goofing off in the stairwells. "just let me down with my Labatt, 44 ounces is where it's at" summed it up well. I would entertain our gang with Indian ragas played only on the high E string of my guitar. I would often do acid at night in my bedroom on alpine while alone. It was great but not so great in Amsterdam when suffering from a nervous breakdown. I was panicking and couldn't stand to be with myself. I'd walk around and wait for my plane back to London to go home. I would drink beer, smoke cigarettes and hang around parks with my back length long hair.

When I finally returned home I found I had a bad rash. I was gone 3 weeks. At my dentist, at the time, some woman said "how sad to have lived your whole entire life at 20 "is one of the remarks I remember. My other best friend, since early on, was Ronnie a drummer I played with in bands and our connection was mostly musical but he was my best friend. His cousin, Allan, was a good bass player and we would often jam the 3 of us, the good old days. I only played guitar at the time unlike now where I play mandolin, pedal steel, guitar and a little banjo and excluding banjo, play them all well. Also, simultaneously, I began my lifelong therapy with psychiatrists starting with dr. John Unwin at the Allan memorial.

The only relief I had was Librium or valium and I had many demons. It was obvious my future was tied in with music but because of my parents, denied myself this lifetime vocation. Instead I was petrified about ending up in a hospital which I finally did in about 2002 at the Allan for 5 days. It was there that they changed my medication to what I still take now in 2021. I later saw dr. Pivnicki, former prime minister of Canada's father-in-law. I had seen all types of therapists beginning in my early 20's, many of which my father booked for me. Getting back to Ronnie, he always said I owed him six years of lifts as he frequently was our wheels. Another musical friend was Emil. I was his lead guitarist. Still another was Dennis, who I would meet with at Beaver Lake on the mountain every summer. He was one of the best musicians I ever played with. He was from Vermont and although I didn't know it at the time, he must have been a draft dodger as it was the time of the Vietnam war. People would love to listen to us at beaver lake and we had our own repertoire. Mitsumi Takahashi, the news commentator in Montreal, loved us and I think had a crush on Dennis. She was 17 or so at the time. We, my friends and I, were exactly the best age for music almost historically, although every generation thinks their music is the best. The Beatles the stones the grateful dead,

Gordon light foot, Simon and Garfunkel, and Bob Dylan were all the rage and we soaked it up. There was Karen the faghag of Jerry's gay cousin josh.

We would all go to Café Campus, including Karen with whom I had several dates. And Mary Lou, who is now deceased. I had sex with her twice and she was part of our gang also. Mary Lou also played violin and enjoy jamming with us. we were all part of the same Sir George Williams crowd. At this time in my life I was very paranoid especially with my mother. I'd come home from school and was always afraid of being caught doing drugs. Also at Emils house, I would always get drunk and stoned and was also worried when I got home. The story of my life was being attracted to women and being horny and doing nothing about it. Amanda, marina, karen are just 3 examples of frustration and super powerful desires being unfulfilled. I'm still like that even now.

But the one constant in my life was music and guitars, especially Martin's. I remember at about 14, putting ads up and looking through ads in the Montreal star, the best

English newspaper, for guitars and amps. I loved wheeling and dealing and remember in 1966 buying a brand new beautiful Fender mustang for $310 and splitting the cost with my father. I was in heaven. I would go to the pawn shops and bought a Harmony sovereign and a Pyramid 12 string there. I always had a passion for guitars and Jerry and I would go to the Yellow door coffeehouse and be on the lookout for Martin guitars, our choice of acoustic guitars. I, in my life, have had many hundreds of Martin's pass through my hands, some of them worth $100000. It has truly been my great passion, that and playing them, and later on pedal steel guitars and of course mandolins, some of which were worth $140000 US dollars. Having none of these right now leaves me wanting! Speaking of Jerry and his wife Lila brings to mind their wedding and the gift I got for them. which was a lladro statue of a woman. Well I went to Birks downtown and was looking at gifts for them when I saw some nice looking China statues.

As I was looking at them and touching them, another early ritual, four statues fell off the shelf and smashed. I had to go to the manager's office to talk about restitution. I picked one up off the floor whose arm was broken off and proceeded to find a lady who could repair it not too far from Birks. Well I got it repaired and gave the statue to Jerry and Lila as a wedding gift. As it turned out two years later I asked them about the statue and they said that their cat knocked it over and broke it. Funny how things work out. As for getting married that never happened but I had lots of chances. Barbara and later Linda and, at Ogilvie's, carol, all would have tied the knot with me. Barbara, if not actual marriage, wanted to at least get engaged which I wouldn't do. Carols sister told her I was probably her best prospect and she actually confided in me that she had very strong feelings for me but that didn't do it either. I liked Carols companionship but we never had sex or even close to it as I never instigated it, typically just going out together. In other words, nothing came of it.

Also I was beginning to feel comfortable with people my parents age and in particular their friends. I associated my generation and my friends with discomfort and my issues and problems. I wanted to be around old people who weren't a reminder Of myself. Avoiding my problems by avoiding my friends and schoolmates and drugs and drug taking of my generation. Every Thursday afternoon I would go to Bruce Reid's house and exchange guitar lessons for supper with his family. I actually planned my school Schedule around that time on Thursdays. I wanted no reminder of my problems and the girls, drugs and friends wouldn't do especially from my age group. I was definitely a casualty of the drug years. I wanted to escape from my issues as I tried to do with drugs but mostly I would like to be alone. No more drugs but solitary self-confinement, avoiding people and friends except for Emil whom I would visit every Sunday night with my guitar after eating at the Brown Derby a good restaurant and landmark in Montreal. I would take the bus and come home the same way until I stated driving and taking my car. We worked out a repertoire but we never played anywhere, just parties which was the closest we had to a gig. He always said we weren't ready. I missed Emil, as he was extremely talented but never went out to play in public. I heard very recently that he inherited his aunts Stradivarius violin. His not performing was a shame because he played guitar, electric and acoustic piano and harmonica and sang great, and was extremely talented. Like I said, one of the best I've ever known. But mostly I avoided any connection with people that were crazy or anything to do with landing up in a hospital which was my biggest fear.

I was constantly afraid I was going crazy and was scared stiff of being committed to 4 east, the Psychiatric ward in the Jewish general. Also I liked familiar things and repetition like watching the same movies, American graffiti over and over again. The same with the 1970s movies, Jaws and deliverance. I was secure at home with my old father and would escape into that world. When I got kicked out of home I didn't know where to go. I had traveler checks and my father's car. I ended up at chateau versaille downtown on Sherbrooke street which was a hotel, but too expensive and not permanent. At the hotel they were sure I was a tourist as I paid with traveler's checks. I was used to hotels and going away and staying there was familiar. Not so with an apartment.

A couple of days later Emil met me and we walked around looking for an apartment which I didn't want. I was lost but still worked at Ogilvie's which was at least familiar. I always liked the familiar. My next move was to decarie near my father's office and building. I started going to Murray's a family restaurant which was from the past and reminded me of my parents and in addition, was prevently old people. This was a habit that lasted 15 years. Most people there were afraid of me because I yelled and banged and smashed the table. Once I was so out of control I went to the washroom downstairs and kicked the sink, causing a flood which was repeated in the coming years. On decarie, on the 3rd floor of a building, I smashed the toilet and started a real flood, serious enough that the owner of the building drove in from the south shore to check on. In my fathers building near there on decarie in the basement, floods were not unfamiliar caused by me and I would repeatedly call bill the plumber who had his office in the same building on Decarie, as a storefront. Bill once said how can you be crazy like that; all the black tenants are laughing at you. It was a big disgrace and embarrassment which was the truth. Bill ended up buying the building and unlike me, was tough and the tenants were afraid of him. It was in that building near my father's office that I met Katsua kimura from Japan who became my girlfriend and ended up living together in the Americana building on cote St. Luc road. This was a disaster and was the time I started becoming physically abusive with women. We drove to Washington DC, Katsua and me, in my Datsun B-210 from the late 70's. We made it but it was also marked by abuse, both mental and physical. We also went to lake placid a couple of years after the winter Olympic s there. I don't remember much from those trips - I guess I'd rather blank them out. I got that little car, a TV, stereo and skis and a ski rack from one of her friends who were going back to Japan and paid $2000 for everything. That was my first car.

I would go to my dad's office every morning with little to do but it felt comfortable if not happy for me to do it. I would see him every day but I wasn't allowed back at alpine. Things came to a head and my mental illness advanced to my limit on alpine

when I was about 19. My moods were safe and secure and being

protected and following that, angry self-pity and desperation.

The last of the first mood had arrived and I realized I could

continue no longer and I made a superhuman effort to lift

myself out of this routine. I concentrated as much as humanly

possible to pick myself up and even my doctor, a bit later, said

that I had an inner strength and resilience to be able to do this.

That was my first psychiatrist at the Allan memorial

hospital. He said that in order to see him again I would

have to make a big change and go out on my own away

from home but I didn't actually do that until I was thrown

out at 27. But before that I thought I'd find that change

in Atlantic city. Where I was staying was a small kind of a

hotel run and owned by a family from New Jersey. One of

the family was a man named john fields and he was a singer

guitarist and, as I had my harmony sovereign guitar with

me, we began to play together. He was so impressed with

my lead guitar playing he continued to write me letters for a year after I returned home, beseeching me to come to silver spring Maryland to stay with him and play. He didn't forget about me and thought my playing perfectly complemented his singing and playing. He was also a song writer and tried playing with other accompanists only to see I was what he needed. I think, at this point of my life, I was probably at the peak of my musical powers at the age of 22. But whenever I got close to playing somewhere I'd cop out. That happened early on in university when I was playing acoustic guitar in a little group with Allan, Marty, and a good chick singer playing folk and blues. I was creative, spontaneous and had the uncanny ability to follow any kind of song hearing it for the first time. I always avoided playing in public though and was terrified of this. Getting back to my home environment, I wish I kept better pictures of the damage I caused where I lived. I have only one picture from decarie and one from my townhouse On Richmond Avenue.

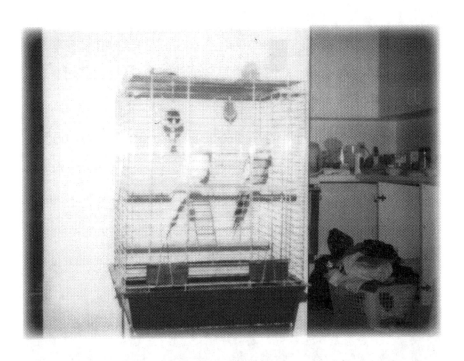

A musical guy came over once and commented on there being no kitchen cupboard doors as I had broken every single one and when Ronnie came over he asked me why there were no doors on any of the rooms. Also all of them were smashed. Glass especially was so breakable and represented my fragile state of mind. But while windows were broken other types of glass, such as mirrors light fixtures and drinking glasses were too. I still literally bear the scars on my right hand and arm. John fields was surprised when he visited my fathers office where I lived and stated "what a hole". My dream, going back to the early 80's, was to have a nice place with nothing smashed. Even on decarie, at the height of destruction, I would buy nice things like furniture and Knick knacks and dishes and stereos because I liked nice things before they were broken. TVs, radios and stereos were no match for my destructive prowess. I used to drive to the West Island to construction sites to visit model homes and dream of living there. I did that repeatedly. To get away from Decarie I dreamt of being in nice surroundings which led me to buying a brand new townhouse near downtown, in the borough of St. Henri. It was fresh, just completed. I went to the electronics store, Magic touch on Queen Mary and bought 2 window air conditioners to complete the package but the dream was short lived. As some guy told me more gyrock and material came out that went in. Entire walls were demolished and it was easy to break because the gyprock that they used for indoor walls was 3/8", very thin, not like the plaster walls on decarie and buildings of older construction. In my basement apartment on decarie, my friend Morrie called it Berlin 1945.

One time in that basement apartment a Lebanese woman, of a family that hated me, told Helen Taylor the tenant above me, that at night when I made an incredible amount of noise from kicking the walls as hard as I could, to call the police who'd witness the noise and probably evict me. Well I heard a car door close and thought it might be the police, and stayed completely quiet so their plan didn't work out inducing Helen to say it was my freaky radar. Another time in that apartment, a big crazy dope smoking Rastafarian tried to smash down my door. If he got in he very likely could have killed me.

The altercation began when he parked in the one little driveway in front of the building. I got so mad I parked in back of him making it impossible for him to get out. I believe it was in him at the very least, to beat the shit out of me. I called the police who told him loudly the parking spot was mine and I then moved my car. Much later in about 2002 I did end up in the Allan mental facility for a stay of 6 days. I freaked out, was out of control and smashing things and my friend Julie called 911 and they came with an ambulance for me and took me to the Jewish general hospital. But they quickly moved me to the royal Victoria to access me. They changed my medication, which helped a lot and I was fine. I'm lucky for my short stay as some seriously sick patients are there for 6 months or even longer. Before that I was seeing Dr. Linda Riven who I became aggressive with and she did me no good anyway. Just prior I put my arm through my glass kitchen window and got 8 stitches and later on had an operation for the injury.

This was a low point for me in the last 25 years. Still fresh in my mind was the shadows of my window shades appearing to be like prison bars. This was on Cranbrooke avenue in cote St. luc near the Americana apartments. I still think one of the worst days of my life was walking along with other movers from the Americana to my new apartment on cranbrooke. It was a very hot day and with my rituals, walking back and forth, it was unbearable. With my rituals and repetitions getting dressed in the late 70s and early 80s was torturous. It would literally take a half an hour to put on, take off, put on my clothes until I whipped myself into a frenzy. Only anafranil, the anti- depressant drug, later give me some modicum of relief.

The rituals were so bad they paralyzed me with obsessive compulsive actions which were completely out of control. With the frustration and anger I would kick the walls repeatedly and break things. On the way to Murray's on Queen Mary

I would move stones and things on the ground, going back and forth, until it was perfect. Always counting in my head. When the green light came on I would cross, but nothing like a normal person would, as it had to be just so. Maybe retracing my steps 10 times. At the time I was oblivious to reality and what was going on around me I was so involved with my rituals. I got so frustrated that I screamed. Also touching things, poles trees and cars and always infernal counting was unbearable. People naturally would stare at me and by the time I reached Murray's I was exhausted and ranting and yelling both inside the restaurants and on the streets. In fact, I got little relief from these horrible rituals until I moved to NDG in 1985. I bought a detached house which was my salvation as nobody was around and I no longer had to make as much noise being afraid of the neighbor's reaction.

Sometimes I would walk to Queen Mary to the royal bank, my dad's bank. I would make rent cash deposits there. Around this point I was playing in a country band with 3 other guys but I was the only real musician, they would say.

I had a problem with Mike, the bass player. I would resent giving him lifts up to Lachute and back but I never voiced my disapproval, the story of my life- keeping my feelings to myself. In Lachute, the rest of the band would stay over but I would drive home and return the next night. It was a surprise to them that I was the only one to actually keep the pay as their bar bill was always more than their pay. Funny! When I was in this band I was living on Cranbrooke next apartment to a big scary older guy. I felt the need, due to my illness to kick the walls at night always testing which I did whenever people could hear me. Anyway. Because of this, he would terrorize me by going outside and banging my window paralyzing me with fear. One time I called the police on him, only to be told by the cop "If you woke me up I wouldn't just threaten you, I would kill you".

One time he chased me outside with what looked like a gun. Later on he smashed the back side window of my Datsun B-210. Another time I went to a local McDonald's where I got into a shouting match with a group of kids who then waited outside for me. One of them punched me in the face and knocked me down. It was a strong looking black guy who came to my rescue, broke it up, picked me up, and told me to leave, which I did. I will now tell you how on decarie, in the basement, I was robbed repeatedly. 4 times I would return to that basement apartment only to find my front door kicked open. The thieves, 3 local kids, were aware of my habits and how much noise I would make smashing and kicking everything. They knew nobody would pay any attention to them breaking in. The last time they robbed me they were caught loading my possessions into a car. In the 4 robberies they stole my valuable guitars, cameras, stereo equipment and $5000 cash of rent money I had collected from the tenants. I was happy when I moved out. I remember at this low point in my life, yelling "There is no God ". Before this I was jamming with a group of college kids in Westmount in one of their parent's houses. This situation was little more than an excuse to get drunk and party. One night I kept going to the kitchen for beer but, because of my rituals with glass, would bite down on the glasses and crack them. I did this with about half a dozen glasses. When the kid's parents came home the next day they asked what happened with all the missing glasses.

But in a detached house that was not the case. I still broke things and made noise on the streets but not to the extent I did before. One problem I had was hitting cars front windshields at just the right spot on the glass to crack them. One BMW car I had had windshield replaced 10 times plus the mirror mounted on the windshield was always broken off. I got a frequent customer discount at Lebeau auto glass. Not so long ago, 20 years ago at a low point I hit the back window of an unmarked car outside the police station just as the female cop came out of the station. She caught me doing it. She was pissed and of course didn't understand. She said if you do this again you will be in a cell. Another time I was parked on Somerled avenue and tried to cross the street but it wasn't just right so I crossed back and hit the back car window of my car until it was ok to go on. A store owner witnessed me hitting my car and thought it wasn't mine and I might have a been trying steal it or vandalize it so they called the police s responding with 3 cop cars. I told them the bmw in question was in fact my car and then tried to explain about obsessive compulsive rituals. One of the cops understood about OCD and let me go. At the Jewish general parking lot, a little before, at another low point about in 2002. A little later I was going out with a really crazy girl named Marcella. My main memory of her was a trip we took in her car to Malone New York to pick up a very valuable 1939 Martin guitar. When we got to the house in Malone Marcella started, or should I say, continued drinking and became unruly. She sat there with her legs apart and asked the people if they could see her crotch.

This type of lewd behavior continued until we left. The real trouble began after more drinking, when she stopped the car and told me to get out in the middle of New York State. I grabbed my guitar, a $75000 Martin guitar, my passport and a six pack of beer. I then took a taxi to the us border and proceeded to pass by customs on foot, luckily with my passport. When I explained to the customs officer that I had a fight with my girlfriend he told me to go inside to call a taxi to Montreal, and $200 later that was the end of that saga. A little before that in about 2004, I was very agitated at an appointment with my therapist at the Jewish general hospital. I was trying to walk around after Dr. Ron brown could see I was in a bad state. He told me to walk around thinking I'd calm down. But I only became more agitated, yelling and hitting everything in the parking lot. I hit the front windshield of an ambulance and cracked it. Nobody saw me. Then I got a taxi and was so keyed up and with the strength of extreme anxiety, in the back seat, I, broke off the window crank. But once again I was lucky and the driver didn't see me. I broke the Handle completely off. Another time on Somerled I went into a bank and got angry and frustrated with the bank machine and punched the window of the outside door and completely smashed it. When I left the bank a woman on the street said did you just break that window? But once again nobody arrested me and I wasn't caught. I was lucky again. Luckily the camera didn't betray me and I got away with it. It is interesting to note with this myriad of rituals I was always counting. Counting my steps, counting how many times I touched something and counting just the right number of times I took to cross the street all the time getting the right number or I couldn't continue.

Certain numbers like 6 were safe and others to avoid were 4 and 9. One time in university a friend told me about a guy he knew, who was studying numerology in school, who cracked up and saw numbers everywhere in store windows. He was committed to a psychiatric hospital. If the fear of this J wasn't so significant to me I wouldn't go on remembering it. I was petrified of the same thing happening to me. Especially when I lived in the basement on decarie and after on Richmond, my go to repairman was Raymond. He worked for and was a friend of my father. He used to occupy the apartment my father had his office in and was the janitor. After my father died Raymond would be constantly fixing my walls. In fact, I once told him I would write this book of memoirs and title it gyprock and he thought that would be perfect. He would be with me mostly putting panels and sheets of gyprock up. It was strange and made little sense to be putting up fresh walls every day only to kick them in so quickly. And repeat the process. Finally, Raymond had had enough and refused to keep coming. When Raymond was janitor there was a young guy living above that would be breaking things and throwing fits, not unlike I would do later. He was crippled and thought everyone was looking at him. His father would consult my father, a doctor and was very worried about his son. We felt sorry for the family and had little fear the same behavior would come home to me. Anyway, when I realized my dream at first of a nice home in my townhouse on Richmond in 1984, Raymond starting coming again.

I, in fact, have a picture in which an entire wall of new gyprock was being put up. You can see an empty wall awaiting its new panel of gyprock. These memories are the grist of this book and am only too glad to say, with medication, effort and age, I am no longer living in a broken home both figuratively and literally. Gyprock, is after all, a fitting title and Raymond would think it perfect.

After university I didn't do much but a couple of years after, maybe a year or two, I got a job at miracle mart in the Cavendish mall. It became a pattern, getting fired from jobs began there, and after about 3 months I did actually get fired. The actual event bringing this about was putting a low price on a toy for a man who told me he didn't have enough money to buy it, so I took my price gun and put a lower price on it. When he went to the cash to pay for it the manager noticed the toy Tonka truck was priced lower than it should have been and the manager asked the man who sold it to him and he pointed me out. I was fired right then and there. I worked in the toy and sports section same as I did a couple of years later at Ogilvy's department store downtown on St. Catherine street. That job lasted longer, almost 2 years. These jobs I was getting, being a store clerk, were not what I went to 5 years of university for, and they certainly not what I wanted to do. I was filling in time and treading water with these jobs and had nothing to do with my musical talents on the guitar. I spent my time at Ogilvy's lusting after women and hanging around different departments where there were pretty women like the cosmetics and perfume section. My heart and head were not in it and it was an effort to stay there. I have dreams even now of trying to get my job back and in my dreams Raymond Mont petit, the manager of the toys, sports and garden furniture, agrees to take me back again, to go through the motions of working there.

My coworkers were really characters, most of them, and in my department the most interesting was Albert Aikman, a 50-year-old man who was interesting in that he had lots of money and was definitely not working there for the pay. He worked there for many years and wore a dirty rumpled old suit and clothes he never changed. John became the assistant managerial job which Albert believed should have been his as he was there for much longer than john. This created bad blood between the two of them and culminated in a physical confrontation, but albert never got over the slight of being overlooked for the promotion to assistant manager. Staff would come and go at Ogilvy's and at Christmas time when the store got busy, part timers were hired and, like I said, most of them were characters. I was in it for the girls and Carol, who I have mentioned elsewhere in this book, was working full time. I saw her socially outside of the store and we'd go drinking after work and go to parties. Many of my coworkers and myself would go down the street to the Rex tavern after work and the Irish Lancer, another bar close by. Boredom at the store would overcome us and we would joke around and kibitz among ourselves to break the monotony and it was in fact a wonder I wasn't fired much sooner. I would constantly come in late in the morning after nights of drinking and I avoided work as much as possible and would hang around waiting to see the girls pass by.

All the girls at the store would come down to the basement where I worked, several times a day as the basement was where the cafeterias were. They would be there for their breaks and lunch. My time there was to socialize and there was one girl in particular i was in love with. Lynn was an Italian beauty I became enamored with and we had as much of a relationship I was emotionally capable of, which was not enough. I should have married her and I think of her often even now forty years later. She was a registered nurse and was just working at Ogilvy's for extra money while going to school to become a nurse. I took her to our country house with my father, the three of us, a few times and it was wonderful. I threw a fit one night at supper at her house and rushed off rudely and for her, that sealed my fate. Soon after, she met an American doctor and they were married and moved to the United states. I never got over her completely and even went so far as to phone her mother in Montreal less than ten years ago, to ask about her. I'm sure she succeeded where she moved to and when she was about 30 I ran into her father one time who informed me she had just got her master's degree in nursing. This was one of my regrets almost the equal of me not going to silver spring Maryland to play music with my buddy John from Atlantic city.

Some years later in the 1980s I became a real estate agent, another job I didn't succeed at and again was fired from. The one thing, however, I was good at was making appointments and cold calling on the telephone. I excelled at this and worked with ester green, a closer, with whom we got listings. The relationship with Esther soured when we got an expensive listing and she resented the idea of splitting 50 50, per our agreement, with me because of one phone call, my crucial call that set up the appointment. In my time as an agent I double ended one sale and my entire 2 years netted me 4 thousand dollars, including one referral. I worked at three companies, royal lepage, century 21 and remax but spent 90% of the time watching other agents getting listings and making sales. I would look at houses I liked, mostly detached homes.

Later I discovered another thing I was good at which was buying and selling vintage musical instruments. I quit real estate and discovered I could actually make money doing this as opposed to watching other real estate agents making money. It was in my blood and this time I was successful. Soon after,

I joined a country band where I played pedal steel guitar, an instrument I took up one summer vacation at Ogilvy's. We played all over. I was taking music courses at night and met a fabulous girl. It was the best time of my life. I was really doing well. Better than any time before. There were 2 times in my life when I lived with a girl, one with my Japanese girlfriend during my decarie days, and one with this fabulous girl who was really out of my league. This time it was at my home on Beaconsfield I had bought in 1985, following my nightmare in my townhouse on Richmond. But this time I was a bit better off emotionally. This situation lasted exactly 9 months and because this girl knew martial arts, I broke my habit of being physically abusive with women too. Just at this time I was taking concrete steps to face my abusive behavior with a workshop for abusive men, many of whom were in prison. So I was a new man and although I was still destructive it was far less and, being in a detached house, I could live a normal life with almost no trouble with neighbor's.

My cousin, Harry Echenberg, who was actually my father's

nephew even though he was seventy, worked with me looking after the real estate my father owned before his death in 1982. Harry also took care of my mother so I didn't have to see her much, which was still very difficult. My father was a slumlord and his buildings by and large were in bad shape, sometimes set on fire by the tenants. We gradually disposed of most of these buildings and it was a relief to be rid of them. We sold the place on decarie I talked about and this was the end of an era. The last property we sold, was, to my present regret, and our country house. This was a mistake as I often miss it and the many good times and great memories I have of it.

Printed in the United States
by Baker & Taylor Publisher Services